For grandma,

who inspires us to love everyone

and embrace our differences.

Written by

Eden Molineux

Illustrated by

Nathalie Beauvois

My name is Alex.

I like to play soccer with

my friends and ride dirt bikes

with my dad.

I'm really good at helping my mom with my sister. I'm also pretty good at magic tricks.

Sometimes, I stutter.

My speech can sound sort of bumpy,

and it's hard for me to get

the words out.

When I stutter, it can be frustrating.

It takes more time for me to talk,

and it stops me from saying the things

I really want to tell people.

It's not easy when people interrupt me or

try to finish my sentences.

When they tell me things like

"slow down" or "take a breath,"

it usually doesn't help.

It hurts when others

laugh at me.

Sometimes,

I'd rather not talk at all.

It helps me when others look at me while I'm talking. When they give me time, I feel like they are listening. I want people to focus on what I say and not how I say it.

It helps when my teacher asks

me what's comfortable.

My speech pathologist is helping

me learn to speak more smoothly.

I'm also learning that it's

okay to stutter.

I would like others to get to know

me and listen to the meaning

behind my words.

Even though I may stutter,

I have a lot to say!

CPSIA information can be obtained
at www.ICGtesting.com
Printed in the USA
BVHW020046011021
617801BV00002B/76